820330

The Monster Book of ABC Sounds

To Tom, Tom, Joe,
Caroline & Tom

First published in the United States 1991 by
Dial Books for Young Readers
A Division of Penguin Books USA Inc.
375 Hudson Street
New York, New York 10014

Created and produced by
David Bennett Books Ltd.,
St Albans, England

Library of Congress Cataloging in Publication Data
Snow, Alan.
The monster book of ABC sounds / by Alan Snow.
p. cm.
Summary: Rats and monsters play a game of hide-and-seek
in this alphabet book of sounds.
ISBN 0-8037-0935-8
1. English language—Alphabet—Juvenile literature. 2. Sounds,
Words for—Juvenile literature. [1. Alphabet. 2. Sound.]
I. Title
PE1155.S58 1991
421'.54—dc20 90-39384 CIP AC

The Monster Book of A·B·C Sounds
by Alan Snow

Dial Books for Young Readers

New York

The hide-and-seek game
is about to begin....

Aa

The door is ajar
and the rats go right in.
(This monster wasn't quite ready.)

Bb

A monster pops out
from behind a small door,

Boo!

Hh

This ticklish young monster
is found by his feet.

Another poor monster
splashes down and away.

L l

Three monsters are found
by the sound of their song.

Mm

And this one finds honey,
which doesn't last long.

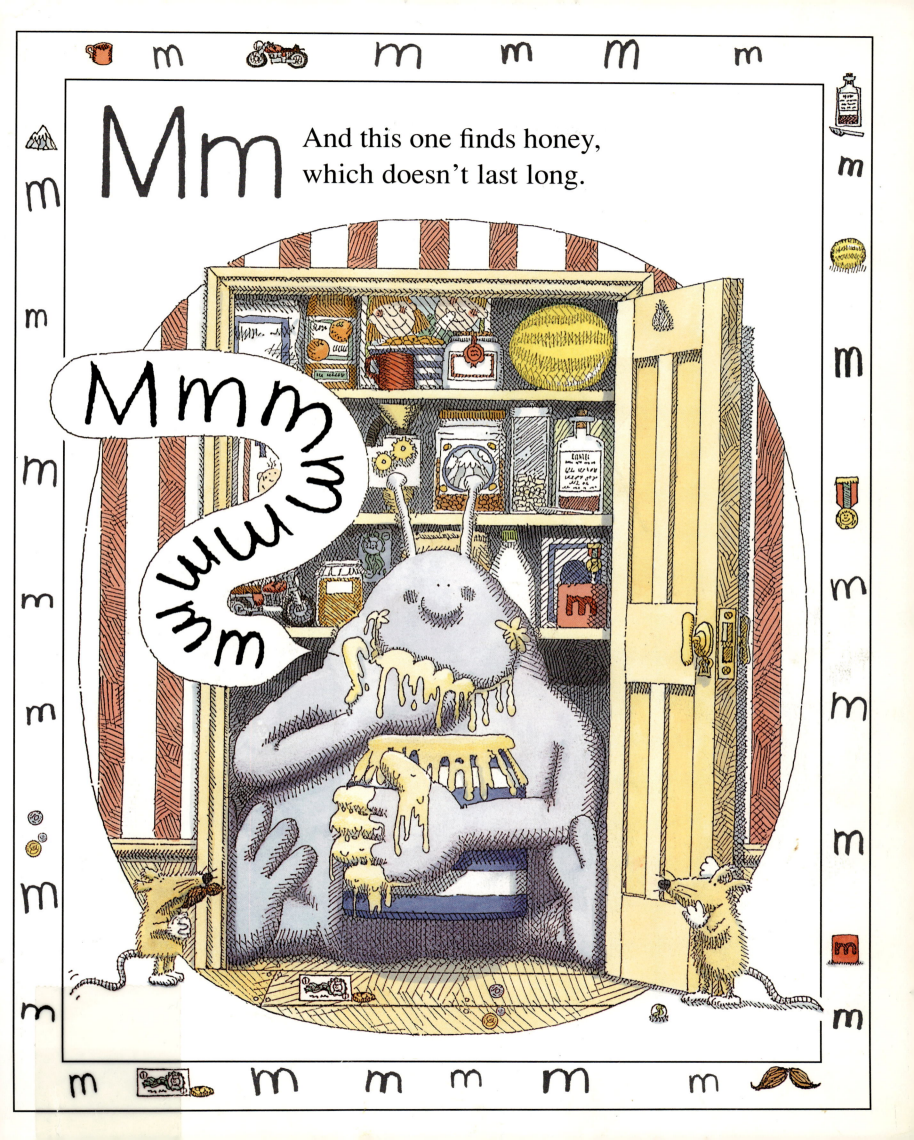

Nn

A very bold monster zooms down just for kicks.

Neeeeaaaw!

He flies upside down
and does other brave tricks.

OoOOooh!

P p

One of the monsters
runs right out of luck.

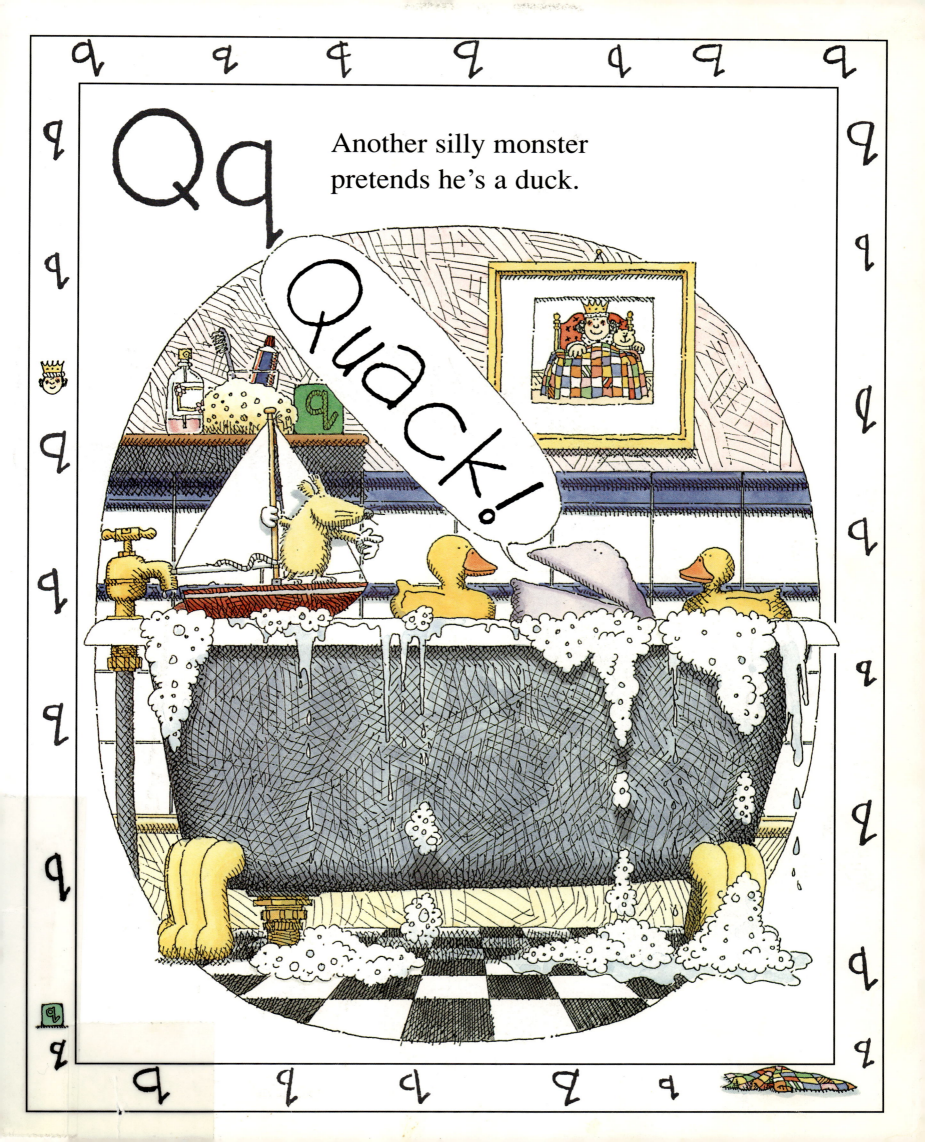

Another silly monster pretends he's a duck.

Rr

The hairiest monster
is big, bad, and mean.

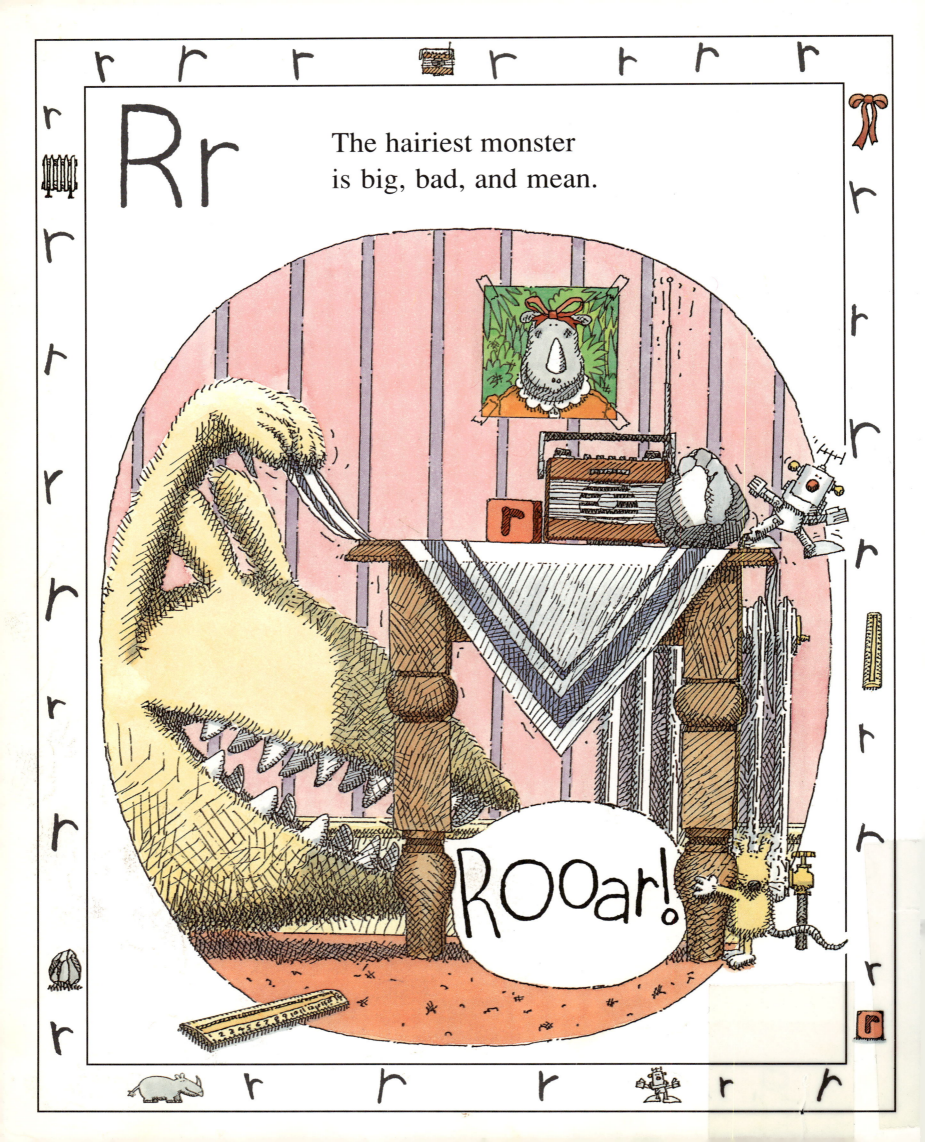

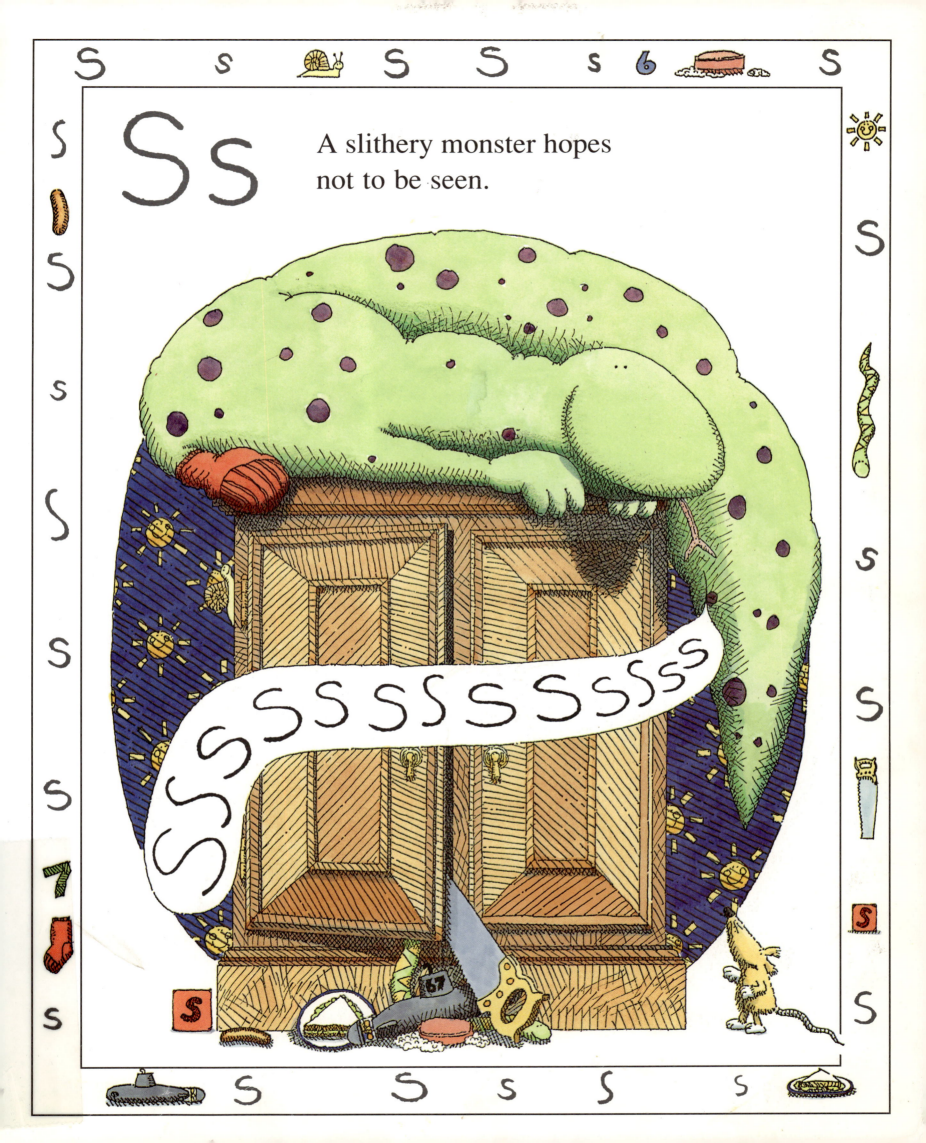

Ss

A slithery monster hopes
not to be seen.

Tt

This monster is gasping
with hunger and thirst.

Uu

He goes to the cabinet,
but rats got there first.

V v

"I bet you can't catch me!"
is this monster's boast.

Vrrrooom!

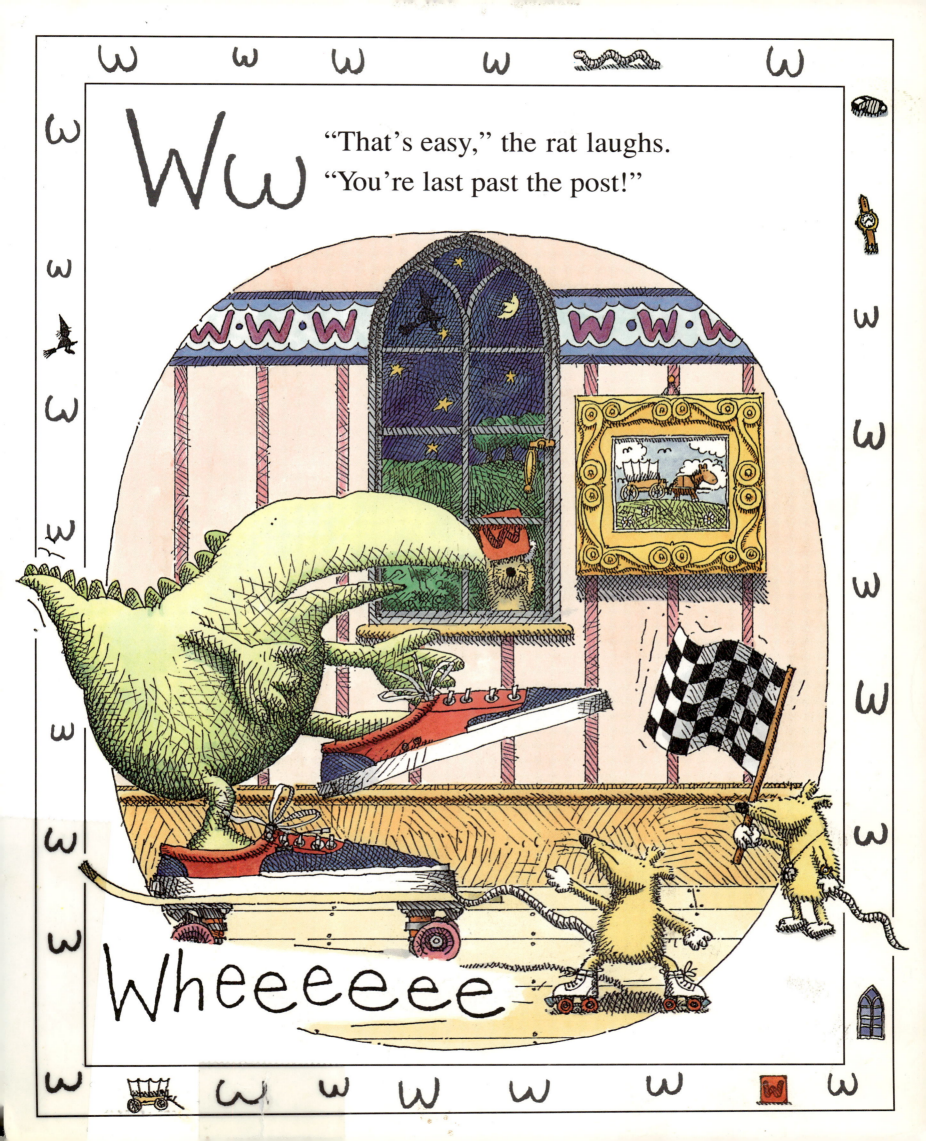

Ww

"That's easy," the rat laughs.
"You're last past the post!"

Wheeeeee

The game is now over and wasn't it great?

They all cuddle up, as warm as can be, and dream of their monster hunt— A through Z.